P9-CMK-813

The Colony of Connecticut

Susan Whitehurst

The Rosen Publishing Group's
PowerKids Press™
New York

LIBRARY
FRANKLIN PIERCE COLLEGE
RINDGE, NH 03

For Megan

Published in 2000 by The Rosen Publishing Group, Inc.
29 East 21st Street, New York, NY 10010

Copyright © 2000 by The Rosen Publishing Group, Inc.

All rights reserved. No part of this book may be reproduced in any form without permission in writing from the publisher, except by a reviewer.

Photo Credits: pp. 1, 7, 8, 11, 12, 15, 19 CORBIS-Bettmann; p. 4 © CORBIS/Michael Maslan Historic Photographs; p. 16 © Library of Congress, Washington D.C./Superstock; p. 20 CORBIS; p. 22 CORBIS/Robert Holmes.

First Edition

Book Design: Andrea Levy

Whitehurst, Susan.
      The colony of Connecticut / by Susan Whitehurst.
            p.   cm. — (The library of the thirteen colonies and the Lost Colony)
      Includes index.
      Summary: Follows the history of the colony of Connecticut, including its daily life, the interaction of the settlers and Indians, and the political struggle to be free of English rule.
      ISBN 0-8239-5479-X
      1. Connecticut—History—Colonial period, ca. 1600–1775—Juvenile literature. [1. Connecticut—History—Colonial period, ca. 1600–1775.] I. Title.
      II. Series. W55
   F97.F66 1999 2000
   974.6'02—dc21

                                                                                                98-32370
                                                                                                   CIP
                                                                                                    AC

Manufactured in the United States of America

Contents

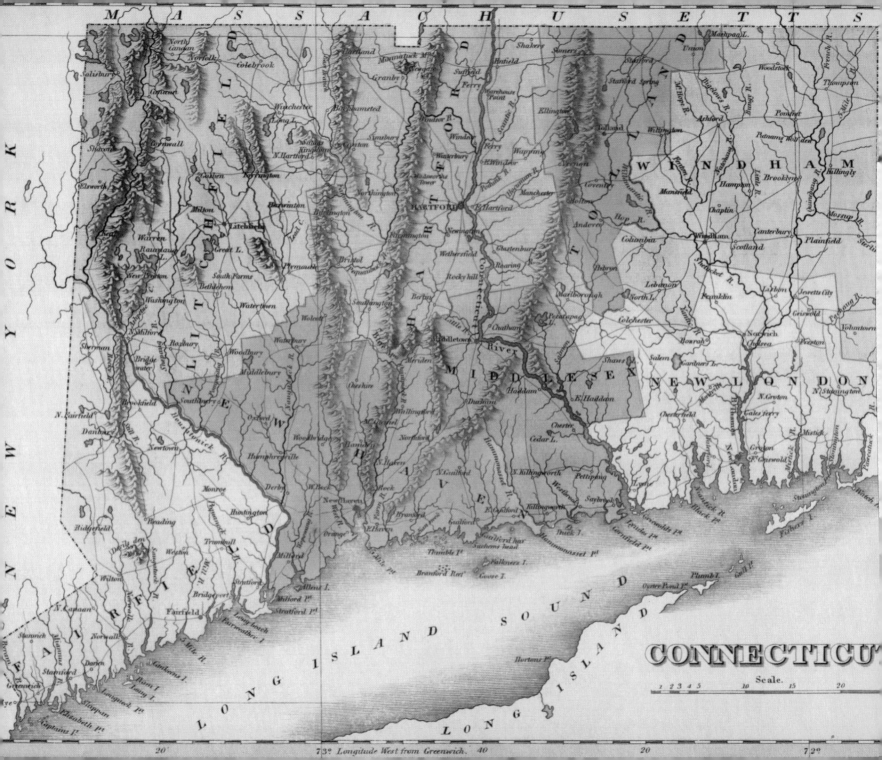

Explorers in Connecticut

The United States began as a handful of **colonies**. In the 1600s, **explorers** from Europe came to Connecticut. A man from the Netherlands named Adriaen Block was the first European to explore Connecticut. In 1614, he sailed up a river that the Algonquian Indians called Quinnenhtukqut, which means "Long River." Block claimed the land for the Netherlands. Block was like many explorers from Europe. He found a **wilderness** area and said that the land now belonged to his country. It didn't matter that other people were already living there. The name Quinnenhtukqut was hard for the colonists to say. Later, they changed it to Connecticut.

Today, the state of Connecticut covers 5,544 square miles, including areas of land and water.

5

The Settlers Arrive

After Block claimed Connecticut for the Netherlands, the Dutch (people from the Netherlands) came and built a trading post, called the House of Hope, in 1633. The Dutch traded with the Algonquians for furs. The furs were shipped back to Europe to make hats and coats.

At the same time, many settlers from Massachusetts decided to move to Connecticut. The new colony had lots of farmland, timber for shipbuilding, and rivers and bays for fishing. Some of the first colonists came in the cold winter of 1635. Ships with their food and supplies could not get up the frozen Connecticut River. The Indians gave them food until spring. Until the colonists built houses, some lived in **dugouts**. A dugout was a hole dug in a hillside that had a roof made of tree trunks and bark.

Furs were weighed before they were traded to figure out how much they were worth. ▶

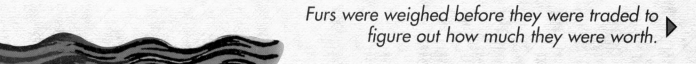

Whose Land Is This?

The colonists often bought land from the Indians. In 1638, land in New Haven County, Connecticut, was purchased from the Quinnipiac Indians for 24 coats, 12 spoons, 12 hatchets, 12 hoes, 24 knives, 12 bowls, and some scissors. The Indians didn't understand the selling of land. They thought land was free, like air. They thought they were agreeing to share the land, but the colonists thought that land was something to be bought and sold. They believed that once you bought a piece of land, no one else could live there.

The Indians were surprised and angry when the colonists told the Indians to move off their land. The Indians were forced to leave their homes and travel farther and farther into the wilderness.

When the European colonists arrived, Quinnipiac Indians lived in the area that would become Connecticut. Mohegan and Pequot Indians also lived in the area.

A New Idea

Soon thousands of settlers came to Connecticut. Three towns on the Connecticut River, Windsor, Hartford, and Wethersfield, joined to make the Connecticut Colony.

Thomas Hooker had led 100 settlers from Massachusetts to Hartford because Massachusetts was too crowded and the Puritan laws too strict. At the time Puritan lawmakers in Massachusetts believed they had the right to tell people what to do. Hooker said that it was the people who should tell the lawmakers how to run the colony. In 1639, the Connecticut Colony approved Hooker's ideas, called "The Fundamental Orders." These laws ruled the colony until 1662.

The ideas in the Fundamental Orders later became an important part of the Declaration of Independence and the Constitution.

This historical picture shows Thomas Hooker leading settlers in a prayer of thanks for their safe arrival in Connecticut. ▶

A Charter for Connecticut

In 1662, the colonists in Connecticut were worried that Massachusetts or New York might try to take over Connecticut. John Winthrop, Jr., the **governor** of Connecticut, sailed to England to ask King Charles for a **charter**. This official piece of paper would say that the colonists had a right to stay in Connecticut. King Charles gave the Connecticut colonists a charter. Two years later the king changed his mind and gave Connecticut to his brother James, the Duke of York. Connecticut remained an English colony for the next 100 years.

King Charles didn't know much about American geography. He wrote in the charter that Connecticut would stretch from the Atlantic to the Pacific Ocean. That would be 3,000 miles!

◀ *John Winthrop, Jr. got a charter for Connecticut from England's King Charles.*

13

Making a Living

Connecticut colonists farmed, fished, and built ships. There was little money in the colonies. People would trade, or **barter**, for the things they couldn't make themselves. Farmers brought extra eggs and vegetables to town and traded them at the general store for sugar, spices, tools, and guns. **Peddlers,** nicknamed Yankee peddlers, visited the colonists who lived in the country. The peddlers loaded their carts with household goods like pots, pans, cloth, shoes, spices, pins, hats, and combs, and traveled from one home to the next.

Craftsmen built ships on Connecticut's coast. The ships were used for fishing and whaling. The ships also took wood, food, and cattle to other countries and brought back guns, spices, and clothes to the people in Connecticut.

Here is a Yankee peddler with his wagon loaded with goods for sale. ▶

14

Making a New Nation

By the 1760s, Connecticut and the other colonies were doing well and making money. The English government wanted some of that money, so it demanded that the colonists pay more **taxes**. The colonists hated the taxes and most refused to pay them. The tax on tea made the colonists in Boston so angry that they tossed tons of tea into Boston Harbor on December 16, 1773. The English closed the harbor until the colonists paid for the tea. With the harbor closed, ships couldn't get into Boston to bring food. For months, colonists from Connecticut, New York, and Rhode Island helped the people in Boston by sending them wagons full of corn, beef, and sugar. Now the colonists were working together. They began to think of themselves as Americans, not colonists.

◀ *Colonists showed their anger about the tax on tea with an event that became known as The Boston Tea Party.*

Unfair Taxes

The more they thought of themselves as Americans, the less the colonists liked paying English taxes. They would say, "No taxation without **representation**!" This meant that the colonists wanted to have a say in how the colonies were being run before they'd pay taxes. England's leaders didn't want the colonists interfering in the way the colonies were run. They just wanted the colonists' money. The English sent soldiers, called Redcoats, to scare the colonists into paying their taxes. It didn't work. England refused to lower the taxes or open Boston Harbor. England and the colonies couldn't agree. In 1774, leaders from Connecticut and the other colonies met in Philadelphia. For two months, they discussed what should be done about the problems with England.

The English soliders were called Redcoats because of the
red coats that they wore as part of their uniforms. ▶

The Revolutionary War

If war broke out, Connecticut wanted to be ready. Towns stored up guns and gunpowder and Connecticut's **militia** trained hard. On April 19, 1775, the American Revolutionary War began in Massachusetts. When the news reached Connecticut, 3,600 members of the Connecticut militia rushed to Massachusetts. Although no major battles were fought in Connecticut, more than 30,000 Connecticut soldiers and sailors fought in the war. When the war ended, every colony was asked to approve the **Constitution**. In 1788, Connecticut approved the Constitution, becoming the fifth state in the new country, the United States.

A Connecticut man named Joseph Martin wrote a book about the war. He wrote that he and other soldiers slept in the rain and snow without a fire. Their shoes wore out from walking, and they walked barefoot through the snow.

◀ *Minutemen were American farmers and workers specially trained to fight at a moment's notice.*

Connecticut Yesterday and Today

The Connecticut navy did its part during the Revolutionary War, capturing 500 English ships. Connecticut's David Bushnell built America's first **submarine**, The Turtle, to help the war effort. Ships and the sea played a big part in Connecticut's past. You can take a peek into that **naval** history at Mystic Seaport (pictured above) in Mystic, Connecticut. Here, you can see historic ships from the time of the Revolutionary War. An early nineteenth-century village is also **re-created** in Mystic, where the history of early America is kept alive.

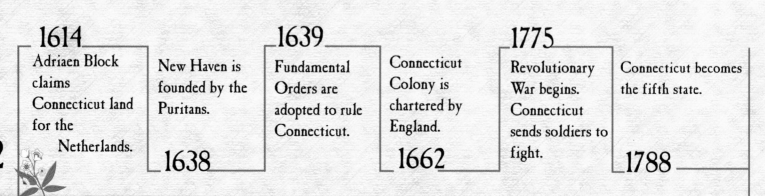

1614 Adriaen Block claims Connecticut land for the Netherlands.

New Haven is founded by the Puritans. **1638**

1639 Fundamental Orders are adopted to rule Connecticut.

Connecticut Colony is chartered by England. **1662**

1775 Revolutionary War begins. Connecticut sends soldiers to fight.

Connecticut becomes the fifth state. **1788**

Glossary

barter (BAR-tur) To trade.

charter (CHAR-tur) An official paper giving someone permission to do something.

colonies (KAH-luh-neez) Areas in a new country where large groups of people move who are still ruled by the leaders and laws of their old country.

Constitution (KAHN-stih-too-shun) A paper that explains how the United States government works.

dugouts (DUG-owts) Homes dug into the ground or the side of a hill.

explorers (ik-SPLOR-urs) People who travel to different places to learn more about them.

governor (GUH-vuh-nur) An official appointed to carry out laws.

militia (muh-LIH-shuh) A group of people who are trained and ready to fight, but are not the army.

naval (NAY-vul) Having to do with ships and shipping.

peddlers (PED-lurs) People who travel around and sell things.

re-created (REE-kree-ay-tid) Built to look like something from the past.

representation (reh-prih-zen-TAY-shun) When people are elected to the government to do what the voters want them to do.

submarine (SUHB-muh-reen) A machine, like a closed ship, for getting around underwater.

taxes (TAK-siz) Money that people give the government to help pay for public services.

wilderness (WIL-dur-nis) An area that is wild and has no permanent settlements.

Index

Web Sites:

You can learn more about Colonial Connecticut on the Internet:
http://www.cslnet.ctstateeu.edu/museum.htm